Spotlight on the 13 Colonies
Birth of a Nation

THE COLONY OF
CONNECTICUT

Richard Alexander

PowerKiDS
press™

NEW YORK

Published in 2016 by The Rosen Publishing Group, Inc.
29 East 21st Street, New York, NY 10010

Editor: Katie Kawa
Book Design: Andrea Davison-Bartolotta

Photo Credits: Cover, pp. 6–7, 12–13, 17 North Wind Picture Archives; p. 4 Universal History Archive/Getty Images; p. 5 alexpro9500/Shutterstock.com; pp. 8–9 Stock Montage/Getty Images; pp. 10, 11 © Meghan Louise/ anotherwalkinthepark.wordpress.com; pp. 14–15 MPI/Stringer/Getty Images; p. 16 (both) Everett Historical/ Shutterstock.com; p. 18 courtesy of the Library of Congress; p. 19 Kean Collection/Getty Images; p. 20 Laura Stone/Shutterstock.com; p. 21 Pete Spiro/Shutterstock.com; p. 22 VectorPic/Shutterstock.com.

Cataloging-in-Publication Data

Alexander, Richard.
The colony of Connecticut / by Richard Alexander.
p. cm. — (Spotlight on the 13 colonies: Birth of a nation)
Includes index.
ISBN 978-1-4994-0314-5 (pbk.)
ISBN 978-1-4994-0335-0 (6 pack)
ISBN 978-1-4994-0344-2 (library binding)
1. Connecticut — History — Colonial period, ca. 1600-1775 — Juvenile literature. 2. Connecticut — History — 1775-1865 — Juvenile literature. I. Title.
F94.3 A449 2016
974.6'02—d23

Manufactured in the United States of America

CPSIA Compliance Information: Batch #WS15PK: For further information contact Rosen Publishing, New York, New York at 1-800-237-9932.

Contents

The First Settlers. 4

Early Settlements 6

War with the Pequot 8

The Colony's Economy. 10

The Fundamental Orders. 12

War and Taxes 14

Protesting the Stamp Act. 16

Revolution! 18

Connecticut Patriots 20

The Fifth State. 22

Glossary 23

Index. 24

Primary Source List. 24

Websites 24

The First Settlers

Native Americans lived in the area that would become the colony of Connecticut long before Europeans arrived. The modern Pequot and Mohegan tribes were among the Native Americans who settled in the Connecticut River valley. The Pequot and Mohegan were a single tribe when Europeans first settled along the Connecticut River. The members of this tribe grew corn, beans, and other crops in the Connecticut soil.

The first European explorer to sail up the Connecticut River was a Dutch sea captain named Adriaen Block. In 1614, he sailed into the Long Island Sound and later reached the Connecticut River. He sailed 60 miles (97 km) up the river, past what would later become the city of Hartford. After Block explored the Connecticut River, the Dutch set up trading posts along its shores. English settlers from Plymouth Colony—in an area that would become part of Massachusetts—then did the same. These European traders built relationships with the Native Americans already living in Connecticut.

Uncas, a leader of the Mohegan tribe

The land that became the colony of Connecticut is located along the north shore of the Long Island Sound. Both the Long Island Sound and the Connecticut River played important roles in Connecticut's history.

Early Settlements

The colony of Connecticut was formed from many early settlements and separate colonies established throughout the 1600s. In 1633, Dutch traders built a **fort** at the mouth of the Park River, which branched off the Connecticut River near what would become the town of Hartford. Two years later, the British founded the first settlement in the area, when John Steele led 60 colonists to that location.

In 1636, Thomas Hooker and Samuel Stone led a group of around 100 British **Puritans** to the town. The next year, the settlement was officially given the name Hartford, after Stone's birthplace of Hertford, England.

Saybrook was another settlement established around the same time as Hartford, between 1635 and 1638. It was its own settlement, set up by John Winthrop Jr., until it joined with the Connecticut settlement. In 1665, the settlements along the Connecticut River joined with the colony of New Haven to form one united colony.

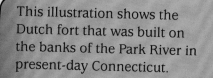

This illustration shows the Dutch fort that was built on the banks of the Park River in present-day Connecticut.

War with the Pequot

For a time, there was peace between settlers in Connecticut and the Native Americans who had been living there long before Europeans arrived. However, that changed as settlements began to grow in Connecticut. The relationship between British settlers and the Pequot tribe became especially uneasy.

In 1636, an armed conflict broke out between settlers and members of the Pequot tribe. This conflict became known as the Pequot War. Settlers from both Massachusetts and Connecticut took up arms against the Pequot.

By the spring of 1637, 13 colonists and traders had been killed by the Pequot. Colonial leaders, led by Captain John Mason, decided to strike back with an attack on a Pequot village in the area that's now known as Mystic, Connecticut. Joined by Mohegan warriors, this group set fire to the village. Over 500 Pequot men, women, and children were killed. The Pequot War ended not long after that, with very few members of the tribe left alive. Those who survived became slaves or escaped to join other tribes.

This **engraving** shows the settlers attacking the Pequot village in 1637.

The Colony's Economy

The economy of Connecticut was **influenced** by its location along bodies of water. The first settlers of Connecticut were farmers, but fishing was also common from the time when the area was only home to Native Americans. Along the coast of the Long Island Sound, there were successful fishing businesses. Colonial Connecticut also had a growing shipbuilding industry.

John Winthrop Jr. played a large role in the growth of Connecticut's economy by introducing mills to the colony. Around 1650, Winthrop built a gristmill on his land in the town of New London. A gristmill uses the power of moving water to grind grain. The **abundance** of water in Connecticut made it easy to get the waterpower needed to run mills in the colony. Winthrop's original gristmill was one of the first **industrial** centers in Connecticut, and people can still visit it today to see how it helped Connecticut's economy grow in its earliest days.

millstones

The Old Town Mill in New London, shown here, is a restored version of Winthrop's first gristmill. The mill Winthrop built was burned down during the American Revolution.

The Fundamental Orders

Unlike most colonies, the government of Connecticut wasn't set up by a **charter** from the British king. Instead, the colony created its government. In 1639, the religious leaders of the colony wrote the Fundamental Orders of Connecticut. This was the first written constitution in what would become the United States. It was made up of a **preamble** and 11 orders that stated the purpose of government and the way the colony should be governed. The Fundamental Orders set up a government where one governor was elected along with six **magistrates**. Because this constitution was written by Puritan leaders, it stressed the importance of religion in the colony.

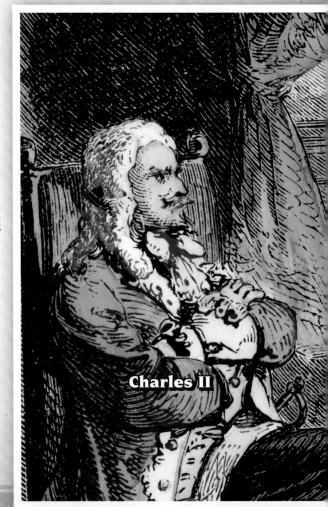

Charles II

The Fundamental Orders was the official constitution of the colony until 1662. That year, Connecticut was given a royal charter from King Charles II of England. This made it a royal colony, or a colony under control of the British king and **Parliament**. John Winthrop Jr. was named the first governor of Connecticut after it received its royal charter.

Charles II was king of England when Connecticut became a royal colony.

War and Taxes

Although Britain had control over Connecticut and other royal colonies, it didn't always rule with the heavy hand that led the colonies to fight for independence. That started after the French and Indian War. This war lasted from 1754 to 1763. It was fought between the British and their Native American **allies** and the French and their Native American allies. The French and Indian War was the North American part of a war that was also being fought between these countries in Europe at the same time.

The British won the French and Indian War. However, fighting the war was expensive. It was also going to cost Britain a lot of money to keep soldiers in the colonies to keep peace between colonists and Native Americans. In order to pay for all this, Britain began to raise taxes in the colonies. These new taxes were very unpopular throughout the colonies, including Connecticut.

During the French and Indian War, Britain borrowed money from other countries. One of the reasons Britain raised taxes in Connecticut and other colonies was to get money to pay back these countries.

Protesting the Stamp Act

After the French and Indian War, Parliament passed acts to increase taxes and tighten Britain's control on the colonies. In 1765, Parliament passed the Stamp Act. This act put a tax on paper goods and dice. The colonists felt they shouldn't be taxed by acts such as the Stamp Act without proper representation in Parliament. They began to protest the Stamp Act and boycotted, or stopped buying, British goods.

The General Assembly of Connecticut wrote a letter to Parliament, stating why the Stamp Act and other taxes were unfair. Colonists in Connecticut and throughout the 13 colonies also formed groups called the Sons of Liberty to fight the Stamp Act. While the Stamp Act was **repealed** in 1766, it wasn't the last act to anger colonists. The more the colonists protested, the more Britain tried to force them to obey. However, the colonists continued to speak out and act against what they felt was unfair treatment by their mother country.

Stamp Act stamps

STAMP
ACT

THE FOLLY OF ENGLAND
THE RUIN OF AMERICA

Shown here is an illustration of a Stamp Act protest in New York. Similar protests were held throughout the colonies, including Connecticut.

Revolution!

Colonial leaders knew the only way to fight unfair British taxes and laws was to join together in protest. In September 1774, colonial leaders met in Philadelphia, Pennsylvania. The group sent letters of protest to King George III of Britain. Connecticut sent Eliphalet Dyer, Roger Sherman, and Silas Deane to represent the colony at what would become known as the First Continental Congress.

On April 19, 1775, fighting broke out between the British and the colonists at Lexington and Concord in Massachusetts. The American Revolution had begun. The colonial leaders knew they were going to need help from France to win the war. In 1776, they sent Deane to France to get money and supplies for their cause. That same year, the Second Continental Congress formally declared the colonies' independence from Britain. On July 4, 1776, the Declaration of Independence was approved. The **colony-states** needed a new government, which was created through the Articles of Confederation. The Articles left much of the governing power in the hands of the colony-states.

This engraving shows a meeting between Deane and two French military officers, Johann de Kalb and the Marquis de Lafayette. Both officers fought alongside the partiots during the American Revolution.

Connecticut Patriots

Connecticut played an important role in America's fight for independence. While it wasn't the **site** of many battles, its location on the Long Island Sound was important for American privateers. A privateer is an armed private ship used by governments during times of war. Privateers that sailed from Connecticut tried to get in the way of British supply ships and helped protect the American coast.

Many men from Connecticut fought against the British in the American Revolution, and some rose to major roles in the American military. Nathan Hale of Coventry, Connecticut, was a spy behind British lines. He was later captured by the British and put to death for spying. He was known for these famous last words: "I regret that I have but one life to lose for my country." Jonathan Trumbull of Lebanon, Connecticut, was governor of the state before and after the American Revolution. He was also a trusted adviser to George Washington during the war.

Nathan Hale Homestead

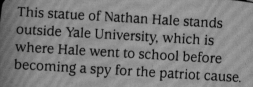

This statue of Nathan Hale stands outside Yale University, which is where Hale went to school before becoming a spy for the patriot cause.

NATHAN HALE
1755–1776
CLASS OF 1773

The Fifth State

The American Revolution ended with the Treaty of Paris in 1783. The new nation was governed by the Articles of Confederation, but the Articles needed improving. In 1787, state leaders came together once again in Philadelphia to strengthen the Articles. They ended up creating a new Constitution, which is how this meeting of leaders came to be known as the Constitutional Convention.

Each state had a different idea of how the states should be represented in the national government. Eventually, Roger Sherman, who was one of the representatives from Connecticut, came up with a compromise now known as the Connecticut Compromise or Great Compromise. It called for a bicameral legislature, or lawmaking body. "Bicameral" means "having two houses." In the legislative branch of the U.S. government, those houses are the House of Representatives and the Senate. Connecticut became the fifth state when it **ratified** the Constitution on January 9, 1788.

Glossary

abundance: A large amount of something.

ally: One of two or more people or groups who work together.

charter: A document issued by a government that gives rights to a person or group.

colony-state: A term for the American colonies when they were no longer colonies under Britain's rule, but not yet truly free and independent states.

engraving: A picture made by cutting an image into a copper plate, forcing ink into the lines of the image, then pressing the plate onto a piece of paper.

fort: A strong building or group of buildings where soldiers live.

industrial: Of or relating to the process of making products by using machinery.

influence: The power to change or affect someone or something.

magistrate: A local official who has some of the powers of a judge.

Parliament: Britain's lawmaking body.

preamble: A statement made at the beginning of something that usually gives the reasons for the parts that follow.

Puritan: A member of a strict Protestant group in England and North America that opposed many practices of the Church of England.

ratify: To formally approve.

repeal: To do away with.

site: Location.

Index

A
American Revolution, 11, 18, 19, 20, 22
Articles of Confederation, 18, 22

B
Block, Adriaen, 4

C
Charles II, 12, 13
Connecticut Compromise, 22
Connecticut River, 4, 5, 6, 7
Constitutional Convention, 22
Continental Congress, 18

D
Deane, Silas, 18, 19
Declaration of Independence, 18
Dutch, 4, 6, 7
Dyer, Eliphalet, 18

F
French and Indian War, 14, 15, 16
Fundamental Orders of
     Connecticut, 12, 13

G
General Assembly of Connecticut, 16
George III, 18

H
Hale, Nathan, 20, 21
Hartford, 4, 6, 7
Hooker, Thomas, 7

L
Long Island Sound, 4, 5, 10, 20

M
Mason, John, 8
Massachusetts, 4, 8, 18
Mohegan, 4, 8
Mystic, 8, 9

N
Native Americans, 4, 8, 10, 14
New Haven, 7
New London, 10, 11

P
Park River, 6, 7
Pequot, 4, 8, 9
Pequot War, 8
Puritans, 7, 12

S
Saybrook, 7
Sherman, Roger, 18, 22
Stamp Act, 16, 17
Steele, John, 6
Stone, Samuel, 7

T
Treaty of Paris, 22
Trumbull, Jonathan, 20

W
Winthrop, John, Jr., 7, 10, 11, 13

Primary Source List

p. 16
Stamp Act stamps. Created by the Board of Stamps. 1765. Ink on paper.

p. 20
Nathan Hale Homestead. Built by Richard Hale. 1776. Wood frame construction. Now located at 2299 South Street, Coventry, CT.

Websites

Due to the changing nature of Internet links, PowerKids Press has developed an online list of websites related to the subject of this book. This site is updated regularly. Please use this link to access the list: www.powerkidslinks.com/s13c/conn